# GOD BLESS AMERICA

### Compiled by Lori Shankle

BARBOUR
PUBLISHING

# GOD BLESS AMERICA

ISBN 1-58660-736-7

Cover image © PhotoDisc, Inc.

Scripture quotations, unless otherwise noted, are taken from the King James Version of the Bible.

Scripture quotations marked NIV are taken from the HOLY BIBLE, NEW INTERNATIONAL VERSION®. NIV®. Copyright © 1973, 1978, 1984 by International Bible Society. Used by permission of Zondervan Publishing House. All rights reserved.

Pieces by Kathi Kolosieke and Kelly Hake are used by permission of the authors.

Published by Barbour Publishing, Inc., P.O. Box 719, Uhrichsville, OH 44683, www.barbourbooks.com

 Member of the
Evangelical Christian
Publishers Association

I pledge allegiance to the flag
of the United States of America
And to the republic
for which it stands:
One nation under God,
Indivisible,
With liberty and justice for all.

# I pledge allegiance
## to the flag
## of the United States
## of America. . .

*Everyone must submit himself*
*to the governing authorities,*
*for there is no authority*
*except that which God*
*has established.*

ROMANS 13:1 NIV

# PLEDGE OF ALLEGIANCE
## HISTORICAL FACTS:

☆ A Baptist minister, Francis Bellamy (1855–1931), wrote the original Pledge in August of 1892.

☆ The original Pledge read: "I pledge allegiance to my Flag and the Republic for which it stands, one nation, indivisible, with liberty and justice for all."

☆ The Pledge was first published in *The Youth's Companion* (September 8 issue), which was a leading family magazine, and the *Reader's Digest*.

☆ Francis Bellamy, who in 1892 was also chairman of a committee of state superintendents of education, prepared a program for the public schools' quadricentennial celebration for Columbus Day. This program was structured around a flag raising and the recitation of his Pledge of Allegiance.

☆ The Pledge's words were changed slightly in 1923 and 1924, when the National Flag Conference decided to replace "my Flag" with "the Flag of the United States of America."

☆ The words "under God" were added to the Pledge by Congress in 1954.

*In* this way we are reaffirming the transcendence of religious faith in America's heritage and future; in this way we shall constantly strengthen those spiritual weapons which forever will be our country's most powerful resource in peace and war.

DWIGHT D. EISENHOWER
1954 speech after Congress
amended the Pledge of Allegiance
to add the words "under God"

# THE STAR-SPANGLED BANNER

O say, can you see, by the dawn's early light,
What so proudly we hail'd at the twilight's last
   gleaming,
Whose broad stripes and bright stars, through
   the perilous fight,
O'er the ramparts we watch'd were so gallantly
   streaming?
And the rockets' red glare, the bombs bursting
   in air,
Gave proof through the night that our flag was
   still there.
O say, does that Star-Spangled Banner yet wave
O'er the land of the free and the home of
   the brave?

O, thus be it ever, when freemen shall stand,
Between their lov'd home, and the war's desolation!
Blest with vict'ry and peace, may the Heav'n
   rescued land
Praise the Pow'r that hath made and preserv'd us
   a nation!
Then conquer we must, when our cause it is just,
And this be our motto—"In God is our trust."
And the Star-Spangled Banner in triumph
   shall wave
O'er the land of the free, and the home
   of the brave.

FRANCIS SCOTT KEY

*We* identify the flag with almost everything we hold dear on earth. It represents our peace and security, our civil and political liberty, our freedom of religious worship, our family, our friends, our home. We see it in the great multitude of blessings, of rights and privileges that make up our country.

But when we look at our flag and behold it emblazoned with all our rights, we must remember that it is equally a symbol of our duties. Every glory that we associate with it is the result of duty done.

CALVIN COOLIDGE

## STARS, STRIPES, AND SACRIFICE

*The* thirteen stripes not only represent the original thirteen colonies that conceived the notion of our freedom, their colors honor our country's greatest men. From basic liberties to sweet justice, etched in those white lines lies the promise of our nation. The lifeblood spilled by our armed forces is mourned in broad red streams across this most recognized badge of American splendor. Every freedom we have shines there, sandwiched between crimson lines of sacrifice.

Our forefathers designated the white stars on a blue field to "represent a new constellation," such as those God placed in the heavens. Together, we create the living legend that a government based on tolerance and freedom can succeed. As the stars draw our eyes toward our heavenly Father, so too American freedom sets the course for other nations.

KELLY HAKE

*Our* Flag carries American ideas,
     American history,
        and American feelings.
Beginning with the colonies, and coming down
to our time, in its sacred heraldry, in its glorious
insignia, it has gathered and stored chiefly this
supreme idea: divine right of liberty in man.
Every color means liberty;
     every thread means liberty;
        every form of star and beam
           or stripe of light means liberty—
not lawlessness, but organized, institutional
liberty—liberty through law, and laws for liberty!

HENRY WARD BEECHER

*A* thoughtful mind,
when it sees a nation's flag,
sees not the flag only,
but the nation itself. . .
the history which belongs
to the nation that it sets forth.

HENRY WARD BEECHER

*Our* brightest hope for the future flutters
from the flag posts of our schools, and we give
no greater tribute than a flag-draped bier. The
promise of tomorrow and our gratitude for
the past are woven
in red's valor,
white's purity,
and blue's limitless horizon.

CATHY MARIE HAKE AND DEBORAH BOONE

*When* freedom from her mountain height
Unfurled her standard to the air,
She tore the azure robe of night,
And set the stars of glory there.

JOSEPH RODMAN DRAKE
*The American Flag*

*Aye,* call it holy ground,
The soil where first they trod,
They have left unstained, what there they found—
Freedom to worship God.

FELICIA D. HEMANS
*The Landing of the Pilgrim Fathers*

## O FLAG OF OUR UNION

O flag of our Union,
To you we'll be true,
To your red and white stripes,
And your stars on the blue;
The emblem of freedom,
The symbol of right,
We children salute you,
O flag fair and bright!

> A poem taught in American classrooms
> nearly a century ago

*Dear Lord,* please help our nation remain united in good times and bad. May we always look to You for guidance as we make decisions that will affect all American people. Bless our leaders, Lord. Give them the knowledge to make wise choices that will benefit our nation. Hold us in the palm of Your hand. Amen.

KELLY WILLIAMS

# . . .and to the republic for which it stands. . .

*My God! How little do my countrymen know what precious blessings they are in possession of, and which no other people on earth enjoy!*

THOMAS JEFFERSON

# OUR THOUGHT OF THEE IS GLAD WITH HOPE

Our thought of thee is glad with hope,
Dear country of our love and prayer;
Thy way is down no fatal slope,
But up to freer sun and air.

Tried as by furnace fires, and yet
By God's grace only stronger made;
In future tasks before thee set
Thou shalt not lack the old-time aid.

Great, without seeking to be great
By fraud or conquest; rich in gold
But richer in the large estate
Of virtue which thy children hold.

With peace that comes of purity,
And strength to simple justice due,
So runs our loyal dream of thee.
God of our fathers! make it true.

O land of lands! to thee we give
Our love, our trust, our service free;
For thee thy sons shall nobly live,
And at thy need shall die for thee.

JOHN GREENLEAF WHITTIER

*These* are the things that remain constant. These are the things that unite us. There are other eternal truths, other eternal constants in our lives: our constant devotion to the principles of freedom, democracy, and the free enterprise system; our constant belief in the promise of this country that the best is yet to come; a country that exists by the grace of Divine Providence—Divine Providence that gave us this land and told us to be good stewards of it and good stewards of each other. The land that God has truly, truly blessed and that we are proud to call AMERICA!

COLIN POWELL
1996 GOP Convention

*The LORD reigns,*
*let the earth be glad;*
*let the distant shores rejoice.*

PSALM 97:1 NIV

## AMERICA, THE BEAUTIFUL

O beautiful for spacious skies,
For amber waves of grain,
For purple mountain majesties
Above the fruited plain!

America, America, God shed His grace on thee,
And crown thy good with brotherhood,
From sea to shining sea.

O beautiful for patriot dream
That sees beyond the years
Thine alabaster cities gleam,
Undimmed by human tears!

America, America, God shed His grace on thee,
And crown thy good with brotherhood,
From sea to shining sea.

KATHERINE LEE BATES, 1893

*We* hold these truths to be self-evident, that all men are created equal, that they are endowed by their Creator with certain unalienable Rights, that among these are Life, Liberty, and the pursuit of Happiness. That to secure these rights, Governments are instituted among Men, deriving their just powers from the consent of the governed.

THOMAS JEFFERSON
The Declaration of Independence, July 4, 1776

After signing of the Declaration of Independence, Samuel Adams commented:

*We have this day restored the Sovereign*
*to whom all men ought to be obedient.*
*He reigns in heaven, and from the rising*
*to the setting of the sun,*
*let His Kingdom come.*

*This* idea that government was beholden to the people, that it had no other source of power is still the newest, most unique idea in all the long history of man's relation to man. This is the issue of this election: Whether we believe in our capacity for self-government, or whether we abandon the American Revolution and confess that a little intellectual elite in a far-distant capital can plan our lives for us better than we can plan them ourselves.

RONALD REAGAN
Speech at the 1964 National Convention

*Who is here so vile that
will not love his country?*

SHAKESPEARE
*Julius Caesar,* III, 2

*Let* our object be our country, our whole
country, and nothing but our country. And,
by the blessing of God, may that country itself
become a vast and splendid monument, not of
oppression and terror, but of wisdom, of peace,
and of liberty, upon which the world may gaze
with admiration forever.

DANIEL WEBSTER

## THE NEW COLOSSUS

Not like the brazen giant of Greek fame,
With conquering limbs astride from land to land;
Here at our sea-washed, sunset gates shall stand
A mighty woman with a torch, whose flame
Is the imprisoned lightning, and her name
Mother of Exiles. From her beacon-hand
Glows world-wide welcome;
her mild eyes command
The air-bridged harbor that twin cities frame.

"Keep, ancient lands, your storied pomp!" cries she
With silent lips. "Give me your tired, your poor,
Your huddled masses yearning to breathe free,
The wretched refuse of your teeming shore.
Send these, the homeless, tempest-tost to me.
I lift my lamp beside the golden door!"

EMMA LAZARUS, 1883

*The* poet called Miss Liberty's torch, the "lamp beside the golden door." Well, that was the entrance to America, and it still is. . . .

The glistening hope of that lamp is still ours. Every promise, every opportunity is still golden in this land. And through that golden door, our children can walk into tomorrow with the knowledge that no one can be denied the promise that is America.

Her heart is full; her torch is still golden, her future bright. She has arms big enough to comfort and strong enough to support, for the strength in her arms is the strength of her people. She will carry on. . .unafraid, unashamed, and unsurpassed.

In this springtime of hope, some lights seem eternal; America's is.

RONALD REAGAN

*Intellectually I know that America is no better than any other country; emotionally I know she is better than every other country.*

SINCLAIR LEWIS

*It* is rather for us to be here dedicated to the great task remaining before us—that from these honored dead we take increased devotion to that cause for which they gave the last full measure of devotion, that we here highly resolve that these dead shall not have died in vain, that this nation, under God, shall have a new birth of freedom, and that government of the people, by the people, for the people, shall not perish from the earth.

ABRAHAM LINCOLN
Gettysburg Address

We have staked the future
of all our political institutions
upon the capacity of mankind
for self-government;
upon the capacity of each and
all of us to govern ourselves,
to control ourselves,
to sustain ourselves
according to the
Ten Commandments
of God.

JAMES MADISON

*Every* thinking man, when he thinks, realizes that the teachings of the Bible are so interwoven and entwined with our whole civic and social life that it would be literally—I do not mean figuratively, but literally—impossible for us to figure what that loss would be if these teachings were removed. We would lose all the standards by which we now judge both public and private morals: all the standards towards which we, with more or less resolution, strive to raise ourselves.

THEODORE ROOSEVELT

*The* fundamental basis of this nation's law was given to Moses on the Mount. The fundamental basis of our Bill of Rights comes from the teaching we get from Exodus and St. Matthew, from Isaiah and St. Paul. I don't think we emphasize that enough these days.

HARRY S. TRUMAN

*If we fail now,*
*we shall have forgotten in*
*abundance what we learned*
*in hardship: that democracy*
*rests on faith, that freedom*
*asks more than it gives,*
*and that the judgment of God*
*is harshest on those*
*who are most favored.*

LYNDON B. JOHNSON
Presidential Inaugural Address
Wednesday, January 20, 1965

*A* nation is formed by the willingness of each of us to share in the responsibility for upholding the common good.

BARBARA JORDAN

*Here is not merely a nation but a teeming nation of nations.*

WALT WHITMAN

*We* shall not fight our battles alone. . . . God who presides over the destinies of nations; and who will raise up friends to fight our battles for us. The battle, sir, is not to the strong alone; it is to the vigilant, the active, the brave. . . . I know not what course others may take; but as for me, give me liberty, or give me death!

PATRICK HENRY

*A* great people has been moved to defend a great nation. Terrorist attacks can shake the foundations of our biggest buildings, but they cannot touch the foundation of America. These acts shattered steel, but they cannot dent the steel of American resolve.

America was targeted for attack because we're the brightest beacon for freedom and opportunity in the world. And no one will keep that light from shining. . . .

None of us will ever forget this day. Yet, we go forward to defend freedom and all that is good and just in our world.

Thank you. Good night, and God bless America.

GEORGE W. BUSH

*The* Founding Fathers made an appropriate choice when they selected the bald eagle as the emblem of the nation. The fierce beauty and proud independence of this great bird aptly symbolize the strength and freedom of America.

JOHN F. KENNEDY

*But they that wait upon the LORD*
*shall renew their strength;*
*they shall mount up*
*with wings as eagles;*
*they shall run, and not be weary;*
*and they shall walk,*
*and not faint.*

ISAIAH 40:31

*The LORD shall command the blessing*
*upon thee in thy storehouses, and*
*in all that thou settest thine hand unto;*
*and he shall bless thee in the land which*
*the LORD thy God giveth thee.*

DEUTERONOMY 28:8

*Father, thank You for Your abundant*
*blessings on this great nation.*
*Please help us to daily remember*
*them and to never take them*
*for granted. Amen.*

RACHEL QUILLIN

*I will make of thee a great nation,*
*and I will bless thee,*
*and make thy name great.*

GENESIS 12:2

## THE AMERICAN'S CREED

*I* believe in the United States of America as a Government of the people, by the people, for the people; whose just powers are derived from the consent of the governed; a democracy in a republic; a sovereign Nation of many sovereign States; a perfect union, one and inseparable; established upon those principles of freedom, equality, justice, and humanity for which American patriots sacrificed their lives and fortunes.

    I therefore believe it is my duty to my country to love it; to support its Constitution; to obey its laws; to respect its flag, and to defend it against all enemies.

WILLIAM TYLER PAGE

*Whensoever* hostile aggressions. . .require a resort to war, we must meet our duty and convince the world we are just friends and brave enemies.

THOMAS JEFFERSON

34

*God's* signs are not always the ones we look for. We learn in tragedy that His purposes are not always our own. Yet the prayers of private suffering, whether in our homes or in this great cathedral, are known and heard, and understood. . . .

America is a nation full of good fortune, with so much to be grateful for. But we are not spared from suffering. In every generation, the world has produced enemies of human freedom. They have attacked America because we are freedom's home and defender. And the commitment of our fathers is now the calling of our time.

GEORGE W. BUSH
National Day of Prayer and Remembrance

*On* this national day of prayer and remembrance, we ask almighty God to watch over our nation and grant us patience and resolve in all that is to come. We pray that He will comfort and console those who now walk in sorrow. We thank Him for each life we now must mourn, and the promise of a life to come.

As we have been assured, neither death nor life, nor angels nor principalities nor powers, nor things present nor things to come, nor height nor depth, can separate us from God's love. May He bless the souls of the departed. May He comfort our own. And may He always guide our country. God bless America.

GEORGE W. BUSH
National Cathedral
September 14, 2001

## . . .one nation under God. . .

*No King but King Jesus!*

One of the rallying cries
of the American Revolution
(from the Boston, Massachusetts,
Committee of Correspondence)

*O Lord,* our heavenly Father, high and mighty King of kings, and Lord of lords, who dost from Thy throne behold all the dwellers of the earth and reignest with power supreme and uncontrolled over all the kingdoms, empires, and governments; look down in mercy, we beseech Thee, on the American States, who have fled to Thee from the rod of the oppressor and thrown themselves on Thy gracious protection, desiring to be henceforth dependent only on Thee. . . . Give them wisdom in council and valor in the field. Defeat the malice of our cruel adversaries. . .constrain them to drop the weapons of war from their unnerved hands in the day of battle.

Be Thou present, O God of wisdom, and direct the councils of this honorable assembly. Enable them to settle things on the best and surest foundations, that the scene of blood may be speedily closed, and order, harmony, and peace may be effectually restored, and truth and justice, religion and piety prevail and flourish among Thy people. . . . All this we ask in the name and through the merits of Jesus Christ, Thy Son and our Savior. Amen.

JACOB DUCHE
First prayer offered in Congress
September 7, 1774

# O GOD, OUR HELP IN AGES PAST

O God, our help in ages past, Our hope for
　　years to come,
Our shelter from the stormy blast, And our
　　eternal home!

Before the hills in order stood, Or earth received
　　her frame,
From everlasting Thou art God, To endless years
　　the same.

A thousand ages in Thy sight, Are like an
　　evening gone;
Short as the watch that ends the night, Before
　　the rising sun.

Time, like an ever-rolling stream, Bears all its
　　sons away;
They fly forgotten, as a dream, Dies at the
　　opening day.

O God, our help in ages past, Our hope for
　　years to come,
Be Thou our guide while life shall last, And
　　our eternal home.

ISAAC WATTS
Based on Psalm 90

*It* cannot be emphasized too strongly or too often that this great nation was founded, not by religionists, but by Christians; not on religions, but on the gospel of Jesus Christ. For this very reason peoples of other faiths have been afforded asylum, prosperity, and freedom of worship here.

PATRICK HENRY

*The* Declaration of Independence first organized the social compact on the foundation of the Redeemer's mission. . . . [I]t laid the cornerstone of human government upon the first precepts of Christianity.

JOHN QUINCY ADAMS
Speech commemorating the
Declaration of Independence
July 4, 1837

*And all these blessings
shall come on thee,
and overtake thee,
if thou shalt hearken
unto the voice of the
LORD thy God.*

DEUTERONOMY 28:2

*Belief* in, and dependence on, God is
absolutely essential.

RONALD REAGAN

*It* is the duty of nations, as well as of men, to own their dependence upon the overruling power of God and to recognize the sublime truth announced in the Holy Scriptures and proven by all history, that those nations only are blessed whose God is the Lord.

ABRAHAM LINCOLN

*Blessed is the nation*
*whose God is the LORD;*
*and the people whom he hath chosen*
*for his own inheritance.*

PSALM 33:12

*It* would be peculiarly improper to omit, in this first official act, my fervent supplication to that almighty Being, who rules over the universe, who presides in the councils of nations, and whose providential aids can supply every human defect, that His benediction may consecrate to the liberties and happiness of the people of the United States. . . . No people can be bound to acknowledge and adore the invisible hand which conducts the affairs of men more than the people of the United States. Every step by which they have advanced to the character of an independent nation seems to have been distinguished by some token of providential agency. . . . We ought to be no less persuaded that the propitious smiles of heaven can never be expected on a nation that disregards the eternal rules of order and right, which heaven itself has ordained.

GEORGE WASHINGTON

The LORD shall greatly bless
thee in the land which the LORD
thy God giveth thee. . .only if
thou carefully hearken unto the
voice of the LORD thy God,
to observe to do all these
commandments which
I command thee this day.

DEUTERONOMY 15:4–5

The
LORD
reigns
forever. . .he will govern the peoples with
justice. Those who know your name will
trust
in you,
for you,
LORD,
have
never
forsaken
those
who
seek
you.

PSALM 9:7–8, 10 NIV

*How priceless is your unfailing love!*
*Both high and low among men find*
*refuge in the shadow of your wings.*

PSALM 36:7 NIV

*In* this situation of this assembly, groping, as it were, in the dark to find political truth. . . How has it happened, sir, that we have not hitherto once thought of humbly applying to the Father of Lights to illuminate our understandings? In the beginning of the contest with Britain, when we were sensible of danger, we had daily prayers in this room for the Divine protection. Our prayers, sir, were heard; they were graciously answered. . . . Have we now forgotten that powerful Friend?

I have lived, sir, a long time; and the longer I live, the more convincing proofs I see of this truth, that God governs in the affairs of men. And if a sparrow cannot fall to the ground without His notice, is it probable that an empire can rise without His aid? We have been assured, sir, in the sacred writings, that "except the Lord build the house, they labor in vain that build it." I firmly believe this; and I also believe that without His concurring aid, we shall succeed in this political building no better than the builders of Babel; we shall be divided by our little, partial, local interests, our projects will be confounded, and we ourselves shall become a reproach and a byword to future ages.

BENJAMIN FRANKLIN

*The* choice before us is plain, Christ or chaos, conviction or compromise, discipline or disintegration. I am rather tired of hearing about our rights and privileges as American citizens. The time is come, it now is, when we ought to hear about the duties and responsibilities of our citizenship. America's future depends upon demonstrating God's government.

PETER MARSHALL, CHAPLAIN
U.S. Senate, 1947–1949

*The* Bible must be considered as the great source of all the truth by which men are to be guided in government as well as in all social transactions.

NOAH WEBSTER

*That Book, sir,
is the rock on which
our republic rests.*

ANDREW JACKSON

*In* no other place in the United States are there so many and such varied official evidences of deep and abiding faith in God on the part of governments as there are in Washington. . . . Inasmuch as our great leaders have shown no doubt about God's proper place in the American birthright, can we, in our day, dare do less?

ROBERT BYRD, 1962

*The heritage of the past
is the seed that brings forth
the harvest of the future.*

Inscribed on the statue "Heritage"
flanking the National Archives Building,
Washington, D.C.

*The Word of God requires
that to maintain the peace
and union of such people,
there should be an orderly
and decent Government
established according to God.*

Fundamental Orders of Connecticut, 1639

*So* great is my veneration of the Bible,
that the earlier my children begin to read it
the more confident will be my hope that they
will prove useful citizens of their country
and respectable members of society.

JOHN QUINCY ADAMS

*The* Bible is endorsed by the ages.
Our civilization is built upon its words.
In no other Book is there such a collection
of inspired wisdom, reality, and hope.

DWIGHT D. EISENHOWER

*Within* the covers of the Bible
are all the answers for
all the problems men face.
The Bible can touch hearts,
order minds, and refresh souls.

RONALD REAGAN

*The* more profoundly we study
this wonderful Book,
and the more closely
we observe its divine precepts,
the better citizens we will become
and the higher will be
our destiny as a nation.

WILLIAM MCKINLEY

*Whatever makes men good Christians
makes them good citizens.*

DANIEL WEBSTER

*A* patriot without religion
in my estimation is as great a paradox
as an honest man without the fear of God.

ABIGAIL ADAMS

52

*It* is impossible to account for the creation of the universe without the agency of a Supreme Being. It is impossible to govern the universe without the aid of a Supreme Being. It is impossible to reason without arriving at a Supreme Being.

GEORGE WASHINGTON

*All* the good from the Savior of the world is communicated through this Book [the Bible]; but for the Book we could not know right from wrong. All the things desirable to man are contained in it.

ABRAHAM LINCOLN

*The* moral principles and precepts contained in the Scriptures ought to form the basis of all our civil constitutions and laws. All the miseries and evils which men suffer from vice, crime, ambition, injustice, oppression, slavery, and war proceed from their despising or neglecting the precepts contained in the Bible.

NOAH WEBSTER

*Human* law must rest its authority ultimately upon the authority of that law which is divine. . . . Far from being rivals or enemies, religion and law are twin sisters, friends, and mutual assistants. Indeed, these two sciences run into each other.

JAMES WILSON
Signer of the Constitution
and an original justice on the U.S. Supreme Court

"If my people,
who are called by my name,
will humble themselves and pray
and seek my face and turn
from their wicked ways,
then will I hear from heaven
and will forgive their sin and
will heal their land."

2 CHRONICLES 7:14 NIV

# GREAT KING OF NATIONS, HEAR OUR PRAYER

Great King of nations, hear our prayer,
While at Thy feet we fall,
And humbly with united cry
To Thee for mercy call.
The guilt is ours, but grace is Thine,
O turn us not away;
But hear us from Thy lofty throne,
And help us when we pray.

Our fathers' sins were manifold,
And ours no less we own,
Yet wondrously from age to age
Thy goodness has been shown.

When dangers, like a stormy sea,
Beset our country round,
To Thee we looked, to Thee we cried,
And help in Thee was found.

With one consent we meekly bow
Beneath Thy chastening hand,
And, pouring forth confession meet,
Mourn with our mourning land.
With pitying eye behold our need,
As thus we lift our prayer;
Correct us with Thy judgments, Lord,
Then let Thy mercy spare.

JOHN H. GURNEY

*We* have been the recipients of the choicest
bounties of heaven. We have been preserved,
these many years, in peace and prosperity.
We have grown in numbers, wealth, and power,
as no other nation has ever grown. But we have
forgotten God. We have forgotten the gracious
hand which preserved us in peace and multi-
plied and enriched and strengthened us; and
we have vainly imagined, in the deceitfulness of
our hearts, that all these blessings were produced
by some superior wisdom and virtue of our own.
Intoxicated with unbroken success, we have
become too self-sufficient to feel the necessity
of redeeming and preserving grace, too proud
to pray to the God that made us! It behooves
us, then, to humble ourselves before the offended
Power, to confess our national sins, and to pray
for clemency and forgiveness.

ABRAHAM LINCOLN
April 30, 1863
Proclamation for a National Day
of Fasting, Humiliation, and Prayer

*There are
a good many problems
before the American people today,
and before me as president,
but I expect to find the solution
of those problems just in the
proportion that I am faithful
in the study of the
Word of God.*

WOODROW WILSON

*O Lord,* when we, Thy children, are apprehensive about the affairs of our world, remind us that Thou art in Thy world as well as above and beyond it. Remind us that Thou art not indifferent. For Thou art not a spectator God, high and lifted up, serene and unperturbed. The feet that were wounded are still walking the trails of earth. The heart that was broken on the tree still feels every human woe.

PETER MARSHALL, CHAPLAIN
U.S. Senate, 1947–1949

*God,* You've blessed America
With riches beyond compare—
Golden fields, glorious skies—
So many beauties rare.

You've given us great freedom
And smiled upon this land,
As our fathers walked beside You
And followed Your commands.

Now, Father, give us wisdom
To walk with You once more,
So You can bless this nation
As You have done before.

RACHEL QUILLIN

# GOD OF OUR FATHERS

God of our fathers, whose almighty hand
Leads forth in beauty all the starry band
Of shining worlds in splendor thro' the skies,
Our grateful songs before Thy throne arise.

Thy love divine hath led us in the past,
In this free land by Thee our lot is cast;
Be Thou our ruler, guardian, guide, and stay,
Thy word our law, Thy paths our chosen way.

From war's alarms, from deadly pestilence,
Be Thy strong arm our ever sure defense;
Thy true religion in our hearts increase,
Thy bounteous goodness nourish us in peace.

Refresh Thy people on their toilsome way,
Lead us from night to never-ending day;
Fill our lives with love and grace divine,
And glory, laud, and praise be ever Thine.

DANIEL C. ROBERTS

# . . .indivisible. . .

*How good and pleasant it is when*
*brothers live together in unity!*

PSALM 133:1 NIV

We the people of the United States,
in order to form a more perfect Union,
establish justice,
insure domestic tranquility,
provide for the common defense,
promote the general welfare,
and secure the blessings of liberty
to ourselves and our posterity,
do ordain and establish this
Constitution for the United States
of America.

Preamble to the Constitution
of the United States

*The* highest glory of the American Revolution was this: It connected in one indissoluble bond the principles of civil government with the principles of Christianity. From the day of the Declaration. . .they [the American people] were bound by the laws of God, which they all, and by the laws of the gospel, which they nearly all, acknowledge as the rules of their conduct.

JOHN QUINCY ADAMS

*Lastly and chiefly, the way
to prosper and achieve good success
is to make yourselves
all of one mind for the good
of your country and your own,
and to serve and fear God,
the Giver of all goodness,
for every plantation which our
heavenly Father hath not
planted shall be rooted out.*

Instructions for the Virginia Colony, 1606

*"You are the light of the world.*
*A city on a hill*
*cannot be hidden."*

MATTHEW 5:14 NIV

*May* God save the Union!
Still, still may it stand upheld
by the strength of the patriot hand,
to cement it our fathers ensanguined the sod;
to keep it we kneel to a merciful God.

From a patriotic hymn

*May the God who gives*
*endurance and encouragement*
*give you a spirit of unity among*
*yourselves as you follow Christ*
*Jesus, so that with one heart*
*and mouth you may glorify*
*the God and Father of our*
*Lord Jesus Christ.*

ROMANS 15:5–6 NIV

☆ ☆ ☆

*United we stand,*
*divided we fall.*

Motto of the State of Kentucky

*The* strength of the Constitution lies entirely in the determination of each citizen to defend it. Only if every single citizen feels duty bound to do his share in this defense are the constitutional rights secure.

ALBERT EINSTEIN

*Scripture* says: "Blessed are those who mourn for they shall be comforted." I call on every American family and the family of America to observe a National Day of Prayer and Remembrance. . . . We will persevere. . . . In time, we will find healing and recovery; and, in the face of all this evil, we remain strong and united, "one nation under God."

GEORGE W. BUSH

*Dear Lord,* although we may not always see eye to eye, please remind us that we are brothers and sisters. We work in different places; we've had different upbringings; we've lived our lives entirely separate from one another. . . . Aside from our differences, Lord, we remain bound by Your love for us as a people and a nation. Amen.

KELLY WILLIAMS

*One flag, one land, one heart, one hand, one nation, evermore!*

OLIVER WENDELL HOLMES
*Voyage of the Good Ship Union*

*Be completely humble and gentle; be patient, bearing with one another in love. Make every effort to keep the unity of the Spirit through the bond of peace.*

EPHESIANS 4:2–3 NIV

# . . .with liberty and justice for all.

*Proclaim liberty throughout all the land unto all the inhabitants thereof.*

LEVITICUS 25:10
Inscription on the Liberty Bell

*You* have rights antecedent to all earthly governments; rights that cannot be repealed or restrained by human laws; rights derived from the Great Legislator of the universe.

JOHN ADAMS

*Liberty cannot be established without morality, nor morality without faith.*

HORACE GREELEY

# AMERICA

My country 'tis of Thee,
Sweet land of liberty:
Of thee I sing.
Land where my fathers died,
Land of the Pilgrims' pride,
From every mountainside,
Let freedom ring.

My native country, thee,
Land of the noble free,
Thy name I love.
I love thy rocks and rills,
Thy woods and templed hills,
My heart with rapture thrills,
Like that above.

Let music swell the breeze,
And ring from all the trees,
Sweet freedom's song.
Let all that breathe partake;
Let mortal tongues awake;
Let rocks their silence break,
The sound prolong.

Our fathers' God to Thee,
Author of liberty,
To Thee we sing.
Long may our land be bright,
With freedom's holy light,
Protect us by Thy might,
Great God, our King.


Our glorious land today,
'Neath education's sway,
Soars upward still.
Its hills of learning fair,
Whose bounties all may share,
Behold them everywhere,
On vale and hill!


Thy safeguard, liberty,
The school shall ever be,
Our nation's pride!
No tyrant hand shall smite,
While with encircling might,
All here are taught the right,
With truth allied.

Beneath Heaven's gracious will,
The stars of progress still,
Our course do sway.
In unity sublime,
To broader heights we climb,
Triumphant over time,
God speeds our way!


Grand birthright of our sires,
Our altars and our fires,
Keep we still pure!
Our starry flag unfurled,
The hope of all the world,
In peace and light impearled,
God hold secure!

SAMUEL FRANCIS SMITH

*The* almighty God has blessed our land in many ways. He has given our people stout hearts and strong arms with which to strike mighty blows for freedom and truth. He has given to our country a faith which has become the hope of all peoples in an anguished world.

FRANKLIN D. ROOSEVELT
Fourth Presidential Inaugural Address
Saturday, January 20, 1945

*Freedom and fear,*
*justice and cruelty*
*have always been at war,*
*and we know that God*
*is not neutral between them.*

GEORGE W. BUSH

*Religion,* morality, and knowledge are necessary to good government, the preservation of liberty, and the happiness of mankind.

U.S. SUPREME COURT, 1892

*Where the Spirit of the Lord is, there is liberty.*

2 CORINTHIANS 3:17

*Liberty,* when it begins to take root, is a plant of rapid growth.

GEORGE WASHINGTON
*Maxims of Washington*

*It is for freedom that Christ
has set us free.*

GALATIANS 5:1 NIV

*The* religion which has introduced civil liberty
is the religion of Christ and His apostles. . . .
This is genuine Christianity, and to this we owe
our free constitutions of government.

NOAH WEBSTER

78

## LET FREEDOM RING

Below her spacious sapphire skies,
Above the cliffs where eagle flies,
Far from the bounds of earthly care,
A cadence rises through the air.

Upon her fields once stained with red,
Beneath the tombs of heroes dead,
Beats a pulse with fervor fine—
A gift from heaven most divine.

Within her countless hallowed halls,
Beyond mere confine of all walls,
There moves a spirit ere unseen,
Yet felt with every heartbeat keen.

God's own grace upon this land,
Foundations built by mighty hand,
Her tenor soars on eagle's wing,
From sea to sea let freedom ring!

KATHI KOLOSIEKE

*We Americans
understand freedom;
we have earned it,
we have lived for it,
and we have died for it.
This nation and its people
are freedom's models
in a searching world.
We can be freedom's missionaries
in a doubting world.*

BARRY GOLDWATER
Speech at the 1964 Republican National Convention

*Freedom* is not a gift bestowed upon us by other men, but a right that belongs to us by the laws of God and nature. . . . I never doubted the existence of the Deity, that He made the world, and governed it by His providence. . . . The pleasures of this world are rather from God's goodness than our own merit. . . . Whoever shall introduce into the public affairs the principles of primitive Christianity will change the face of the world.

BENJAMIN FRANKLIN

*Neither* the wisest constitution nor the wisest laws will secure the liberty and happiness of a people whose manners are universally corrupt. He therefore is the truest friend of the liberty of his country who tries most to promote its virtue, and who, so far as his power and influence extend, will not suffer a man to be chosen into any office of power and trust who is not a wise and virtuous man.

SAMUEL ADAMS

*Protection* and patriotism are reciprocal.

JOHN C. CALHOUN

*Greater love hath no man than this,
that a man lay down his life
for his friends.*

JOHN 15:13

*God* grants liberty only to those who love it
and are always ready to guard and defend it.

DANIEL WEBSTER

*Men must choose
to be governed by God,
or condemn themselves
to be ruled by tyrants.*

WILLIAM PENN

☆ ☆ ☆

*Blandishments* will not fascinate us,
nor will the threats of a "halter" intimidate.
For, under God, we are determined that
whatsoever, whensoever, or howsoever we shall
be called to make our exit, we shall die free men.

JOSIAH QUINCY

*It* is extremely important to our nation, in a political as well as religious view, that all possible authority and influence should be given to the Scriptures, for these furnish the best principles of civil liberty, and the most effectual support of republican government. The principles of all genuine liberty, and of wise laws and administrations, are to be drawn from the Bible and sustained by its authority. The man therefore who weakens or destroys the divine authority of that book may be accessory to all the public disorders which society is doomed to suffer.

NOAH WEBSTER

*A general* dissolution of principles and manners will more surely overthrow the liberties of America than the whole force of the common enemy. While the people are virtuous, they cannot be subdued; but when once they lose their virtue, they will be ready to surrender their liberties to the first external or internal invader. . . . If virtue and knowledge are diffused among the people, they will never be enslaved. This will be their great security.

SAMUEL ADAMS

The God who gave us life
gave us liberty. . . .
And can the liberties of a nation
be thought secure when we have
removed their only firm basis,
a conviction in the minds
of the people that these liberties
are of the gift of God?
That they are not to be violated
but with His wrath?
Indeed, I tremble for my country
when I reflect that God is just;
that His justice cannot sleep forever.

THOMAS JEFFERSON

## BATTLE HYMN OF THE REPUBLIC

Mine eyes have seen the glory of the coming of
     the Lord;
He is trampling out the vintage where the grapes
     of wrath are stored;
He hath loosed the fateful lightning of His
     terrible swift sword:
His truth is marching on.

I have seen Him in the watch-fires of a hundred
     circling camps;
They have builded Him an altar in the evening
     dews and damps;
I can read His righteous sentence by the dim
     and flaring lamps;
His day is marching on.

I have read a fiery gospel writ in burnished rows
     of steel:
"As ye deal with My contemners, so with you
     My grace shall deal;
Let the Hero, born of woman, crush the serpent
     with His heel,
Since God is marching on."

He has sounded forth the trumpet that shall
    never call retreat;
He is sifting out the hearts of men before His
    judgment-seat;
Oh, be swift, my soul, to answer Him! be jubilant,
    my feet!
Our God is marching on.

In the beauty of the lilies, Christ was born across
    the sea,
With a glory in His bosom that transfigures you
    and me:
As He died to make men holy, let us die to make
    men free,
While God is marching on.

JULIA WARD HOWE

*When justice is done,*
*it brings joy to the righteous*
*but terror to evildoers.*

PROVERBS 21:15 NIV

*The* only limit to our realization of tomorrow
will be our doubts of today.
Let us move forward
with strong and
active faith.

FRANKLIN D. ROOSEVELT

90

*Duty is ours;
results are God's.*

JOHN QUINCY ADAMS

*The* price of freedom is eternal vigilance.

THOMAS JEFFERSON

*A nation
has character
only when it is free.*

MME. DE STAEL

*Tyranny* is so generally established in the rest of the world that the prospect of an asylum in America for those who love liberty gives general joy, and our cause is esteemed the cause of all mankind. . . . We are fighting for the dignity and happiness of human nature. Glorious it is for the Americans to be called by Providence to this post of honor. Cursed and detested will everyone be that deserts or betrays it.

BENJAMIN FRANKLIN

*Let* every nation know,
whether it wishes us well or ill,
that we shall pay any price,
bear any burden, meet any hardship,
support any friend, oppose any foe,
in order to assure the survival
and the success of liberty.

JOHN F. KENNEDY

*The future doesn't belong
to the fainthearted;
it belongs to the brave.*

RONALD REAGAN

*Crisis* doesn't build character; it reveals the
character developed in our daily walk.

CATHY MARIE HAKE AND DEBORAH BOONE

*Freedom is the recognition
that no single person,
no single authority or government
has a monopoly on truth,
but that every one of us put
on this world has been put
there for a reason and
has something to offer.*

RONALD REAGAN

*And ye shall hallow the fiftieth year, and proclaim liberty throughout all the land unto all the inhabitants thereof: it shall be a jubile unto you; and ye shall return every man unto his possession, and ye shall return every man unto his family.*

LEVITICUS 25:10

*Hushed* the people's swelling murmur,
Whilst the boy cries joyously;
"Ring!" he's shouting, "ring, Grandfather,
Ring! Oh, ring for Liberty!"
Quickly at the given signal
The old bellman lifts his hand.
Iron music through the land.

G. S. HILLARD
*Franklin Fifth Reader*

*Dear Lord,* thank You for my freedom. Please help me to not take for granted all of the liberties that I have in this country. My prayer is for those who cannot celebrate such freedom—those who are unable to worship You or read Your Word openly. . . . Touch their hearts, Lord, and uplift their spirits. Amen.

KELLY WILLIAMS

*We ask almighty God
to watch over our nation. . .
and may He always
guide our country.*

GEORGE W. BUSH
September 14, 2001